THE LITTLE BOOK OF
DIWALI

First published in 2025 by OH
An Imprint of HEADLINE PUBLISHING GROUP LIMITED

1

Disclaimer:

Cataloguing in Publication Data is available from the British Library

ISBN 978-1-03543-025-3

Compiled and written by: Malcolm Croft
Editorial: Saneaah Muhammad
Designed and typset in Pollen by: Tony Seddon
Project manager: Russell Porter
Production: Marion Storz
Printed and bound in Dubai

HEADLINE PUBLISHING GROUP LIMITED
An Hachette UK Company
Carmelite House, 50 Victoria Embankment, London EC4Y 0DZ

The authorised representative in the EEA is Hachette Ireland, 8 Castlecourt Centre,
Dublin 15, D15 XTP3, Ireland (email: info@hbgi.ie)

www.headline.co.uk www.hachette.co.uk

THE
LITTLE BOOK
OF
Diwali

THE FESTIVAL OF LIGHTS

CONTENTS

Welcome to Diwali!

Feasts, fireworks, friends and family – this five-day "festival of lights" is a two-millennia-old religious and cultural tradition that ignites more than just a lot of pretty lights. It is a time when good vanquishes evil, gods conquer demons, knowledge defeats ignorance and the Indian nation enters a new year with a new harvest and new fortunes. Today, Diwali is the largest multi-faith event in the world, honoured annually by more than one billion joyful and grateful devotees.

From *Dhanteras* to *Bhai Dooj* (the first and final days of the festivities), Diwali is filled with a wealth of time-honoured traditions. Whether it's mantras or prayer rituals, sweets or snacks, decorations or celebrations, each of them keep Diwali'ers smiling from sunrise to sunset.

With a deep-rooted history steeped in Hindu, Buddhist, Jain and Sikh mythology, gods and goddess, holy cows, golden temples and technicolour fireworks, Diwali is the one global holy holiday that has it all – and is set to become even bigger with each new year.

This *Little Guide to Diwali* shines a ray of pure light on this awe-inspiring festival. Its humble aim is to serve as an ideal introductory reader to those wishing to learn more about the festival, as well as celebrate it in all its awesome glory. Consider this your first step to switching on your inner light. So, spark up your *diyas*, unbox your *mithai* and wrap up your *uphaar*, because it's time for the festival of lights to begin.

Shubh Deepavali!

CHAPTER
ONE

A New Moon

The ancient origins of Diwali have been burning bright in the minds of its devotees for more than 2,500 years.

Let's turn the light on... and get the festivities started!

15 August 1947

The day that India gained independence from its British colonial rulers. Despite there being few Diwali celebrations that year – the nation was still healing from its conflicts with Pakistan – India's freedom was the first step in igniting the nation's own inner light and fueling the popularity of Indian customs and traditions abroad.

That year, Diwali was celebrated on the 12 November.

दी पा व लि

Sanskrit for Diwali

"Deepavali"*– the origin of the word "Diwali" – derives from the Sanskrit words *deep* (meaning "light") and *avali* (meaning "row"). Together, Diwali means "row of lights". The five-day event is now commonly celebrated as the "festival of lights".

For more than two millennia, Hindus around the world have placed a row of clay lamps outside their dwellings to help guide their once-exiled gods Rama and Sita back home to the sacred city of Ayodhya.

* "Deepavali" is used in southern India and "Diwali" is mainly used in the north, as well as internationally.

Diwali is celebrated over five days, and each day has its own unique traditions.

Day 1: Dhanteras

The first day of Diwali is celebrated on the 13th day of the lunar month of Kartika in the Hindu calendar. The word *Dhanteras* comes from the Sanskrit words *dhan* (wealth) and *teras* (13th). This day is observed by praying to the goddess of wealth, Lakshmi, by purchasing gold as a sign of good fortune.

Day 2: Choti Diwali

Choti Diwali marks the triumph of Lord Krishna over the demon Narakasura. With rituals and prayers dedicated to the goddess Kali, this day is designed to ward off all evil spirits before the day of Diwali.

Day 3: Diwali

The main celebration! Families gather together for the main prayer ritual, *Lakshmi Puja* (a prayer to Lakshmi, the goddess of wealth), followed by large feasts and fireworks.

Day 4: Govardhan Puja or Annakut

The first day of the Hindu new year sees friends and relatives visit with gifts and best wishes for the season, along with a celebration of Govardhan Hill, a sacred Hindu site in Uttar Pradesh.

Day 5: Bhai Dooj

The final day of Diwali festivities sees a celebration of the sacred bond between brothers and sisters. Brothers visit their sisters, and sisters ceremonially mark their brothers with a *tilaka*, a red spot on their forehead to represent their spirituality.

Amavasya

The Sanskrit term for a new moon, it is considered to be the perfect day for a Diwali celebration. Diwali begins two days before *Amavasya*, on *Dhanteras*, and ends two days after. Each month has a new moon, a period of a couple of days when the moon is between the sun and the Earth and cannot be seen in the sky.

Diwali can be first traced to ancient India more than 2,500 years ago, when farmers first celebrated the end of harvest and reaped their crops. They would then offer praise and gifts to the gods* Brahma (the creator), Vishnu (the preserver) and Shiva (the destroyer) for granting them a good crop.

* Collectively known as Hindu's holy trinity, or Trimurti.

"

How far that little
candle throws his beams!
So shines a good deed in
a weary world.

"

Portia
William Shakespeare, *The Merchant of Venice*, Act V, Scene i

The Golden Mile

Every Diwali, in Leicester, England, more than 40,000 revellers travel to Belgrave Road, also known as "The Golden Mile", to participate in the largest Diwali celebration outside of India. The festivities include the famous switch-on of the "Wheel of Lights", a decorated Diwali Village, food stalls, funfair rides, a laser show, fireworks display, light installation, rickshaws, lantern processions, live musical guests and free-roaming illuminated giants! Throughout the year, The Golden Mile is known for its Indian restaurants, shops and honouring of Indian traditions.

Icons of Diwali #1:
Lord Rama

According to the *Ramayana*, one of Hinduism's most sacred religious texts, Diwali marks the return of Lord Rama and his wife Sita to Ayodhya, a city situated on the banks of the Saryu river in Uttar Pradesh, after defeating Ravana, a 10-headed demon king, and completing 14 years of exile. As Diwali takes place on Amavasya, or new moon, there is no moonlight to guide Rama and Sita on their journey home from exile, so villagers in Ayodhya lit lamps to help the couple find their way home. The lighting of lamps, sharing of food and giving of gifts are all symbols of lights and a triumph over darkness, the core symbols of Diwali.

A popular Rama chant during the day of Diwali is "Om Shri Ramaya Namaha", translating roughly to "Salutations to the Lord Rama".

May the light of Diwali,
Shine forever in your soul,
Bringing joy and prosperity,
Making your spirit whole.

In November 1947, shortly after India gained its independence from British colonial rule, Mahatma Gandhi, known as the "Father of the Nation", delivered his first Diwali message in a bid to spiritually heal the nation from its recent conflicts and colonization.

"

Brothers and Sisters, today is Diwali and I
congratulate all of you on the occasion. It is a
great day in the Hindu calendar. According to
the Vikram Samvat, New Year begins tomorrow.
You must understand why Diwali is celebrated
every year with illuminations. In the great battle
between Rama and Ravana, Rama symbolized
the forces of good and Ravana the forces of
evil. Rama conquered Ravana and this victory
established Ramarajya in India. Only those who
have Rama within can celebrate this victory.
What we need today is the light of love in our
hearts. We must kindle the light of love within.
Then only would we deserve congratulations.
True light comes from within.

"

Diwali is the largest multi-faith celebration in the world. It is enjoyed by Hindus, Jains, Sikhs and Buddhists, with each religion honouring different origins and traditions:

Hindus celebrate the coronation of the god king Rama after his epic battle with Ravana, the demon king of Lanka. It symbolizes the battle between good and evil.

(There are more than 1.2 billion Hindus in the world.)

Jains celebrate Lord Mahavira's attainment of nirvana, on the same day as Diwali.

(There are approx. 5 million Jains in the world.)

Sikhs celebrate the release of Guru Hargobind Ji from imprisonment.

(There are approx. 30 million Sikhs in the world.)

Buddhists celebrate Emperor Ashoka's conversion to Buddhism.

(There are approx. 520 million Buddhists in the world.)

The Birth of Lakshmi

The first day of Diwali, known as *Dhanteras*, commemorates the day the goddess of wealth and prosperity, Lakshmi, was born. Families who pray to Lakshmi are blessed with good fortune for the year. Did you know that Shmi Skywalker – the mother of the most famous character in all modern cinema, *Star Wars*' Anakin Skywalker (AKA Darth Vader) – is named after Lakshmi? Her son's turn to the dark side was inspired by Hinduism's principal concepts of good versus evil.

"

From within or from behind, a light shines through us upon things, and makes us aware that we are nothing, but the light is all.

Ralph Waldo Emerson
The Over-Soul, 1841

In India there are many seasonal festivals that are celebrated. Perhaps the biggest two are the seasonal kick-starters – **Diwali** and **Holi**.

Diwali (October/November)

A festival of lights that focuses on spiritual reflection, prayers and family homecomings that arrives with the reaping of the harvest and the arrival of autumn.

Holi (March)

A festival of colours and joy, which focuses on social unity and playfulness and celebrates the end of winter, the sowing of new seeds and the arrival of spring.

"

No Diwali party is complete
without an abundance of flowers,
delicious food and great music!
But none of this means anything
without the most important
ingredient: having people you
love to share it with.

"

Padma Lakshmi
Indian-American television personality, model and author

Diwali means love, family and celebrations.

Ranbir Kapoor
Indian actor

"

If you want a love message to be heard, it has got to be sent out. To keep a lamp burning, we have to keep putting oil in it.

"

Mother Teresa
Albanian-Indian Catholic nun and saint

Diwaloween

The term used by those who celebrate Halloween and Diwali together, all in one. In 2024 the two annual traditions fell on the same day. While Halloween is always traditionally celebrated on 31 October, Diwali falls on different dates each year because it is dependent on the lunar calendar.

"

Diwali is the festival of lights, and that also stands for the enlightenment of human beings.

"

Anushka Sharma
Indian actress

As the lamps light up
the night,

They drive away the
shadows of fright.

With every flicker and glow,

Our hearts begin to grow.

" Travel light, live light, spread the light, be the light. "

Yogi Bhajan
American entrepreneur, yoga guru and putative spiritual teacher

Diyas

Small oil lamps, traditionally made of clay, which are lit during Diwali to illuminate homes and streets. LED lights are commonly used today, for safety.

2,512,585

The total amount of *diyas* lit at the same time during Diwali 2024 in Ayodhya, a city in the state of Uttar Pradesh, India – a new Guinness World Record.

Guinness World Record officials were present and awarded a certificate to state Chief Minister Yogi Adityanath to acknowledge the record. The feat beat the 2.2 million lit in the year before. Drones in the sky were used to ensure all the lamps remained lit at the same time.

Legislation
S. 7574/A. 7769

The designation number given to amend New York's education law when Diwali was signed into law and declared a holiday for New York City public schools. This happened on 14 November 2023. As of December 2023, New York state had a Hindu population* of more than 200,000 – about three per cent of the total population.

* In addition, there are more than 78,000 Sikhs in New York and more than 50,000 Buddhists.

"

Listen to the inner light; it will guide you. Listen to the inner peace; it will feed you. Listen to the inner love; it will transform you.

"

Sri Chinmoy
Indian spiritual leader

During Diwali's five-day festivities, *diyas* are lit and windows and doors are left open to help the goddess Lakshmi find her way into people's homes in order to bless and protect them.

In addition to this, Diwali celebrators also clean and declutter their homes. As a result, Diwali is a time of increased charitable giving, when clothes and other household items are given as gifts to charity to help the poor and vulnerable.

"

For I can see that in the midst of
death, life persists;

in the midst of untruth, truth persists;

in the midst of darkness, light persists.

Hence I gather that God is Life,
Truth, Light.

He is Love. He is the Supreme Good.

"

Mahatma Gandhi
Indian lawyer, anti-colonial nationalist and political ethicist

धर्मादर्थः प्रभवति धर्मात् प्रभवते सुखं।
धर्मेण लभते सर्वं धर्मसारमिदं जगत्

"

Wealth comes from righteousness,
and from righteousness comes
happiness. Through righteousness,
one can achieve everything as it is
the essence of this world.

"

Lord Rama
Ramayana, Valmiki, 300 BCE

To commemorate the life and legacy of Mahatma Gandhi and to celebrate Diwali, in November 2021 a £5 coin was unveiled by Rishi Sunak, the first ever Hindu Prime Minister of Great Britain.*

This special collectors' coin featured an image of a lotus, India's national flower, alongside one of Gandhi's most famous quotes: "My life is my message".

* Sunak also minted the UK's first ever gold bar depicting Lakshmi – the Hindu Goddess of wealth – for Diwali 2021.

Ladoo

The most popular Diwali *mithai* (sweet) given and shared with friends and family is a *ladoo*. Made with *besan* (gram flour), coconut and *boondi* (fried chickpea flour balls) and flavoured with cardamom, saffron and ghee, these small, rounded sweets make Diwali even more delicious.

"

It is better to light
one small candle than to
curse the darkness.

"

Eleanor Roosevelt
American political figure, diplomat and activist

Ramayana

Composed in Sanskrit sometime around 300 BCE, *Ramayana*, by the poet Valmiki, is Hinduism's greatest epic poem. It tells the life of Rama, the seventh incarnation of the supreme being Vishnu (one-third of Hinduism's holy trinity), his miraculous birth and his conquest to defeat the 10-headed demon king, Ravana. Ravana had kidnapped Sita, the wife of Lord Rama, and exiled Rama from the kingdom.

Rama went to war with Ravana and ultimately defeated him, restoring himself as king on the throne of India's spiritual city, Ayodhya. Rama's journey is the principal Diwali parable of good defeating evil for Hindus.

Aarti

A devotional prayer, or song, sung in praise of Hindu deities such as Lakshmi, Rama, Vishnu or Ganesha and typically performed during Diwali prayers, known as *puja*.

Aartis are chanted while lighted *diyas* are spun in a circular motion. When *aartis* are chanted as a group, it can create a enchanting, calming and even hypnotic ambience.

"

The story of Diwali?
Yeah, sure. I know it. Um.
It all started a long, long
time ago... er... in a galaxy
far, far away...

"

Sanjeev Bhaskar
British-Indian actor, comedian and television presenter

Ayodhya is regarded as one of the seven sacred cities of Hinduism, home not only to Lord Rama and his wife Sita – as told in the epic fourth-century poem *Ramayana* – but also the home of Hinduism itself. Known as the Sapta Puri, these are the seven holiest cities in Hinduism:

Ayodhya – the birthplace of Rama

Mathura – the birthplace of Krishna

Haridwar – located on the sacred River Ganges

Varanasi – a city never abandoned by Shiva

Kanchipuram – a temple city in Tamil Nadu

Ujjain – the site of the Kumbh Mela pilgrimage every 12 years

Dwarka – the town where Krishna ruled as a king

"

Jai Shree Ram

"

A repeated Hindu chant that translates to "Glory to Lord Rama".

Recanted during Diwali rituals, such as the first lighting of the *diyas*, the chant is a symbol of devotion to the Hindu faith and a tribute to Lord Rama, whose triumph over the malevolent demon king Ravana reminds Hindus of the essential and eternal battle between light and dark.

"

Thousands of candles can be lighted from a single candle, and the life of the candle will not be shortened. Happiness never decreases by being shared.

"

Siddhartha Gautama
The Buddha

CHAPTER
TWO

Sweetness & Light

Diwali has a feast of cherished traditions and practices, from prayer rituals to gift-giving. It's a celebration of all that is sweet and good in this world.

And, in this modern era, which is often clouded with darkness and shade, a little bit of light is no bad thing...

Icons of Diwali #2
Lord Krishna

The eighth incarnation of protector deity Vishnu, Lord Krishna is celebrated the day before Diwali on Choti Diwali – or Naraka Chaturdashi, as it's also known. Krishna defeated the demon king Narakasura, an act of courage that ensured the freedom of 16,000 captive women and symbolized good's vital victory over evil.

It is in celebrating Krishna that the tradition of exploding firecrackers and lighting fireworks began, symbolizing the end of darkness with a burst of light.

A popular Krishna chant on Choti Diwali is "Om Shree Krishnaha Sharanam Mamah", translating to "I take refuge in Lord Krishna".

Swarn

In Sanskrit, *swarn* directly translates to "gold", which is often used in Indian culture to symbolize wealth, purity and prosperity.

In Hinduism, gold is associated with Lakshmi, the goddess of wealth, prosperity and abundance. Diwali is celebrated to honour her, and devotees believe buying gold during the festival will invite her blessings into their homes.

Jal Jeera

One of Diwali's most popular drinks,
Jal Jeera – or cumin-flavoured water – is
the perfect refresher to cleanse the palate
before the feast and festivities begins.
Why not try making it at home?

Ingredients

2 tbsp cumin seeds
2 tbsp mint leaves + extra for decoration
1 tsp fresh coriander leaves
2 tbsp lemon juice
½ tsp black salt or ordinary salt
5 cups chilled water
A pinch of sugar

Serves 6

Method

First, grind the cumin seeds to make a
fine powder. Then roast the powder in
a pan until toasted.

Grind the mint and coriander to make
a paste. Mix together the roasted cumin
powder, mint, coriander paste, lemon juice
and salt. Add water and mix.

Season to taste with sugar. Pour into
glasses and adorn with mint leaves.

Icons of Diwali #3
Lord Ganesha

Identified by his iconic elephant head and four arms, Lord Ganesha is widely revered by Hindus, Jains and Buddhists as the bringer of good luck and is worshipped alongside Lakshmi for wisdom and success.

A common Ganesha prayer chant, performed on the main Diwali night, is "Om Vakratunda Maha-Kaaya Surya-Kotti Samaprabha", which translates to "Greetings to Lord Ganesha, who has a curved trunk, a big body and shines as brightly as a million suns".

"

Be a light unto yourself;
betake yourselves to no
external refuge. Hold fast
to the Truth. Look not for
refuge to anyone besides
yourselves.

"

Siddhartha Gautama
The Buddha

"

Lead us from the unreal
to the Real

From darkness to Light

From death to Immortality.

"

Yajnavalkya
Brihadaranyaka Upanishad, 6th century BCE

ॐ श्रीं ह्रीं क्लीं ऐं सौं ॐ ह्रीं क ए इ ल ह्रीं ह स क ह ल ह्रीं सकल ह्रीं सौं ऐं क्लीं ह्रीं श्री ॐ

Om Shmi Maha Lakshmiyei Namaha

On *Dhanteras* and the day of Diwali, celebrators believe that chanting the Lakshmi Mantra 108 times will ensure the goddess blesses you with wealth, happiness and good fortune in the new year.

"

Let us remember that Diwali represents the annual celebration of the victory of the forces of Rama – that is, non-violence and truth – over those of Ravana – violence and untruth.

"

Mahatma Gandhi
Indian lawyer, anti-colonial nationalist and political ethicist

"

Every little candle is a great knight fighting against the darkness! Every time you feel yourself tiny, remember these brave candles!

"

Mehmet Murat Ildan
Turkish writer

Puja

Prayer rituals, or *pujas*, are performed throughout Diwali, and people from different regions offer prayers to different deities on different days.

The central day of Diwali, however, is called *Lakshmi Puja* for a reason – on this day, prayers are offered to the goddess Lakshmi.

"

There isn't enough darkness in all the world to snuff out the light of one little candle.

"

Robert Alden
American Congregational minister

तमसो मा ज्योतिर्गमय

Tamaso Ma Jyotir Gamaya

This famous Sanskrit *shloka*, or song, translates as "Lead me from darkness to light". It is a phrase that is often recited on Diwali to invoke a spiritual awakening in those who speak it.

Rangoli

A colourful and intricate pattern, usually in the shape of a lotus flower, laid flat on living-room floors, in courtyards or outside homes. They are designed with coloured rice flour, sand, powdered limestone and flower petals.

The word *rangoli* comes from the Sanskrit words *ranga* (colour) and *avali* (row). A representation of happiness and positivity, *rangoli* are used to welcome Lakshmi, the goddess of wealth, into homes during Diwali.

In India, it is common for mothers to make *rangoli* and teach the art to their daughters to pass on the tradition.

Samsāra

The word to describe the cycle of birth,
death and rebirth in Hinduism.
Diwali reminds its devotees to transcend
samsāra through knowledge and
spiritual awakening.

The cycle is defined by two central beliefs:

1. Dharma
The righteous path of living, and the
principles that guide one's actions.

2. Karma
The law of cause and effect, and the
consequences of one's actions.

Patakhe

Firecrackers, or *patakhe*, are an indispensable part of Diwali, with many believing the snap, crackle and pop will ward off bad spirits from entering homes. A common brand is Bijili Crackers.

How to say **Happy Diwali** in different languages in distinct regions of India...

Shubh Deepavali	Hindi
Saal Mubarak	Gujarati
Diwali Chya Hardik Shubhechha	Marathi
Deepavali Nalvazhthukkal	Tamil
Tuhanu Diwali diyan boht both vadhaiyan	Punjabi
Shubho Deepaboli	Bengali
Deepavali Subhakankshalu	Telugu

Ubtan

An ancient and traditional Ayurvedic*
remedy, ubtan is a skincare paste. It is
often used in bathing rituals to cleanse,
exfoliate, rejuvenate and beautify the skin
to symbolize the beginning of the festival
– predominantly on the day before Diwali,
Choti Diwali. It is made from a collection
of natural ingredients such as turmeric,
sandalwood and gram flour.

* The traditional Indian system of medicine.

"

Today's the "Festival of Lights" all o'er;

A joyful day for minds and hearts
and souls;

And people throng the Temples to offer,

Prayers, resolving to take better roles.

Today's the triumph of Good over bad;

But what about the wastage in much ways?

True joy is when you see someone
else smile!

True charity gives joy in Heav'nly style.

"

Dr John Celes
"Diwali", 2003

Annakut

The first three days of Diwali are prayer days to invite greater wealth into our lives. The fourth day – New Year's Day – is also known as Annakut. It's a day Hindus pray to Lord Krishna, the eighth avatar of supreme being Vishnu.

Annakut translates to "mountain of food" and is a 56-dish feast prepared and offered to Krishna as a blessing of appreciation and protection and a celebration of the bountiful harvest of nature.

Hindu temples prepare the mountain of food into the shape of Govardhan Hill, a sacred Hindu site that Krishna once lifted with his little finger to protect the people below from torrential rains sent by Indra, the rain god.

"

There are two ways of
spreading light; to be the
candle or the mirror
that reflects it.

"

Edith Wharton
Vesalius in Zante, 1902

"

Diwali is awesome... and there's food... and there's going to be dancing... and... Oh! I got the raddest outfit.

"

Kelly Kapoor
"Diwali", *The Office*, 2 November 2006

Icons of Diwali #4
Lord Vishnu

Husband of goddess Lakshmi and one of Hinduism's holy trinity, Vishnu the preserver is celebrated on Govardhan Puja, the day after Diwali, for his efforts in defeating the demon king Bali and sending him to the netherworld. Bali had threatened the gods with his immense power. A popular Rama chant during Govardhan Puja is "Om Namo Bhagvate Vasudevaye", translating to "I bow to Lord Vasudeva (or Lord Krishna)".

The Hindu calendar is based on the lunar month, which is the time it takes for the moon to orbit the Earth in relation to the sun. Each lunar month is made up of 30 lunar days, which are grouped into two fortnights of 15 days each.

Which lunar month is your birthday?

1. Chaitra	March–April
2. Vaishakh	April–May
3. Jyeshtha	May–June
4. Ashadha	June–July
5. Shravana	July–August
6. Bhadrapada	August–September
7. Ashvin	September–October
8. Kartika	October–November (Diwali!)
9. Margashirsha	November–December
10. Pausha	December–January
11. Magha	January–February
12. Phalguna	February–March

"

Come on! You know I can't
talk to women unless I'm
lit up like Diwali.

"

Raj Koothrappali*
"The Hofstadter Isotope", *The Big Bang Theory*, 13 April 2019

* Raj, played by Kunal Nayyar, a British-Indian, has to "get lit" (consume
some alcohol) before he is able to converse with the opposite sex.

"

[Diwali is] a festival that's held on the darkest night during a dark time of year, which is exactly when we really need light. It's a time when daylight is really dwindling and the days are growing shorter, especially in the northern hemisphere. We are in need of company, and light, and sweets and festivities.

"

Asha Shipman
Director of Hindu Life and Hindu Chaplain for Yale University

Sweet Lassi

The perfect accompaniment to your delicious Diwali dishes and snacks – such as Dahi Vada, spicy samosas, Murukku and Ras Malai – a Sweet Lassi is traditional, essential... and delicious!

Ingredients

500 ml plain yoghurt
250 ml water
4 tbsp sugar
Crushed ice

Serves 6

Method

Put the yoghurt, water and sugar in a blender.
Add ice and blitz the mixture until frothy. Serve.
Add fruits, such as mango or strawberry, for
an extra sweet flavour.

Diwali has evolved over thousands of years. The earliest references to it are written records of fire worship, known as *Agni Upasana*, and lamps, called *deepa*, in the *Rigveda*, an ancient Indian collection of Sanskrit mantras from the Vedic period, 2,500 years ago. These references show the significance of light in Hindu rituals even then.

CHAPTER
THREE

Golden Touch

Diwali is celebrated
all around the world these days,
growing and gaining speed
and devotees with every new year.

It's now a global celebration,
as enjoyable as it is essential to
spreading laughter, love
and light...

"

It's the night of Diwali,
every house is being
illuminated. On this day,
love is in everyone's heart.

"

Rahul Raichand
Kabhi Khushi Kabhie Gham, 2001

The earliest known reference to the word Diwali can be found in the *Harivamsa Purana* via the word *dipalikaya*, meaning "light leaving the body".

The *Purana*, written by Acharya Jinasena in the year 783 CE, is a sacred text to Jainists.

"

It's time to come home to your true
self and become the source of light that
makes everything around you brighter.
Spread love, spread light and bring you
closer to yourself, because no matter
where you are in your life, we all have
the ability to shine our inner light on this
world. Happy Diwali! Let's you and me get
together and light up all the dark corners
of this world. Deal?

"

Kunal Nayyar
British-Indian actor

In 2009, President Barack Obama became the first U.S. president to personally attend Diwali at the White House, Washington, D.C. – a historic moment for American Hindus, Buddhists, Sikhs and Jains.

"

I've been proud to host Diwali celebrations at the White House – and be the first president to light the *diya* in 2009. Today, Hindus, Jains, Sikhs and Buddhists – some of the world's oldest religions – light the *diya* with family and friends. You celebrate life's blessings – the triumph of knowledge over ignorance and good over evil. But Diwali is also a time for prayer and contemplation, to reflect on our obligations to help our fellow human beings, particularly the less fortunate.

"

President Barack Obama
Diwali, 2009

The word "Deepavali" is first mentioned in the *Padma Purana*, one of the 18 major *Puranas*, a collection of Hindu texts that describe ancient Indian society, traditions and geography, which date back to around 1,500 years ago.

Here's the first mention:

Thaile Lakshmirjale Ganga Deepavalyaschaturdasheem

Praatahkaale Tu Yah Kuryath Yamalokam Na Pashyathi

On the Chaturdashi (14th day of the fortnight) of Deepavali, Goddess Lakshmi will reside in oil and the River Ganga in water. Those who use these in the morning will not need to see Yamaloka.

*Vakratunda Mahakaya Suryakoti
Samaprabha, Nirvighnam Kuru Me Deva,
Sarva Karyeshu Sarvada**

O Lord Ganesha, the one with a curved
trunk and a mighty body, as bright as a
million suns, I pray to you to remove all
obstacles from my path and grant me the
blessing of success in whatever I do.

* Chanting this mantra 20 times a day in the days leading up to Diwali
will ensure double the blessings from Ganesha!

"

Darkness cannot drive out
darkness: only light
can do that. Hate cannot
drive out hate:
only love can do that.

"

Martin Luther King, Jr.
American minister and civil rights activist

"

Light attracts light.

"

Warsan Shire
British writer and poet

Diwali is just one of many awe-inspiring festivals observed by Hindus during the year.

January – Makar Sankranti

To celebrate the sun's transit; rites include ceremonial bathing, mass pilgrimages and sun worship.

February/March – Maha Shivaratri

Marks the end of winter; rituals include fasting and meditation.

March – Holi

Festival of colours which marks the end of winter; rites include mass gatherings and getting covered in colourful dry powder and coloured water.

March/April – Rama Navami

Celebrates spring and the birth of Lord Rama; rituals include storytelling around fires.

August/September –
Krishna Janmashtami

Celebration of Krishna; rites include dance
performances, devotional singing and vigils.

August/September –
Ganesh Chaturthi

Celebration of Lord Ganesh; rituals include prayer,
hymns, fasting and athletic events.

September/October –
Navratri & Durga Puja

Like Diwali, an autumn festival; a nine-day
festival celebrated in the northern and western
regions of India.

October/November – Diwali

The festival of lights; involves fireworks, gift-giving,
feasting and worship.

For Buddhists, Diwali is the time
when Emperor Ashoka is celebrated.
Two thousand years ago, during Diwali,
Ashoka the Great became the personification
of the triumph of good over evil when he
gave up his extremely violent ways and
chose a path of peace.

Before converting to Buddhism, Ashoka was
known for his cruel acts, including beheading
more than 500 people (in one day), massacres
of his concubines and brutal tortures.

Ashoka was Emperor of Magadha, an ancient
Indian empire, from 268 BCE until 232 BCE.
His empire stretched from present-day
Afghanistan to present-day Bangladesh. After
his conversion, Ahsoka played an important
role in the spread of Buddhism across Asia.

"

May the partisans of all
doctrines in all countries unite
and live in a common fellowship.
For all alike profess mastery
to be attained over oneself and
purity of the heart.

"

Emporer Ashoka
Former emperor of the Maurya Empire

"

Over the years, my Diwali celebrations have been evolving, with awareness around firecrackers and not wanting to pollute. I've become much more conscious of that. Diwali is now more about friends and family getting together for a nice meal. This year, we're going on a road trip across the country, a long one from Goa to the Nilgiris, with family and some friends. That's also nice – to be in small towns you've never been to, and celebrate Diwali in a different way.

"

Kalki Koechlin
French actress and writer

"

This Diwali let's take the
opportunity to thank the Lord
for the gift he has given us...
Life. May we have the strength
to show our gratitude ask for His
forgiveness and seek His blessings
for happiness.

"

Shah Rukh Khan
Indian actor and film producer

Asatho Maa Sad Gamaya
Thamaso Maa Jyothir Gamaya
Mrithyor Maa Amritham Gamaya

Lead me from untruth to truth;
Lead me from darkness to light;
Lead me from death to
immortality.

Pavamana Mantra
Ancient Indian mantra found in *Brihadaranyaka Upanishad*

The Churning of the Ocean

Known as *Samudra Manthana* in Hindu mythology, the Churning of the Ocean is the origin story of Goddess Lakshmi and a central event in the ever-continuing struggle between the *devas* (gods) and the *asuras* (demons). According to the legend, gods and demons once churned the primeval ocean of milk to obtain the nectar of immortality, known as *amrita*. During this churning, chaos was created and Goddess Lakshmi emerged from the ocean, bringing with her wealth, prosperity and good fortune.

"

Learn to light a candle in the darkest moments of someone's life. Be the light that helps others see; it is what gives life its deepest significance.

"

Roy T. Bennett
The Light in the Heart, 2020

"

Deepavali is here, Deepavali is here
That gorgeous festival of snacks and sweets
Where everyone enjoys a royal feast
When old and young with delight meet
With love and affection all hearts beat.

Diwali is here, Diwali is here
That gracious festival which celebrates victory
The ancient festival of myth and mystery
That is mentioned in both mythology and history
The festival that signals triumph over tragedy.

"

Shyam Pathak
"Deepvali Delights", 2022

Diwali is beloved as a wonderfully snacky celebration, filled with divine side dishes that are easy to make and even simpler to share.

From Indian cheese balls to paneer tikka, dal pakora to pea kachori, onion bhajis to samosa chaat and bhel puri to aloo paratha, there are countless traditional appetizers to count on.

According to top Diwali chef Maunika Gowardhan, the best Diwali foods to share are Hyderabadi biryani, karanji and rajasthani laal maas, accompanied by chai tea and barfi for dessert.

"

OK, these clothes, this holiday, I need to know everything about Diwali.

"

Carrie Bradshaw
"Diwali", *And Just Like That,* 6 January 2022

Every Diwali, Dubai's Burj Khalifa – the world's tallest building, standing at a height of 830 metres! – is illuminated with a dazzling array of intricate patterns, colours and designs to celebrate and pay tribute to the festival of lights. It's a stunning spectacle to see.

"

May God illuminate your
hearts so that you can serve
not only each other or India
but the whole world.

"

Mahatma Gandhi
Indian lawyer, anti-colonial nationalist and political ethicist

Diwali Playlist

Ten Diwali-inspired songs to help kickstart your festive celebrations in style, performed by India and Bollywood's most famous musical superstars...

1. "Diwali" – Vishal Mishra

2. "Diwali Ki Badhai" – Swaroop Khan

3. "Aali Diwali" – Yukta and Satyam Patil

4. "Aaj Ki Party" – Mika Singh

5. "Shubhaarambh" – Amit Trivedi

6. "Aayi Abke Saal Diwali" – Lata Mangeshkar

7. "Aayi Hai Diwali" – Udit Narayan, Alka Yagnik, Kumar Sanu and Ketki Dave

8. "Deep Diwali Ke Jhute" – Kishore Kumar

9. "Mere Tumhare Sabke Liye Happy Diwali" – Vaishali, Surthi, Divya, Suraj, and Sunidhi Chauhan

10. "Deep Diwali Ke Jhoothe" – Mohammed Rafi

"

May the light of
Diwali bring you peace
and happiness.

"

Amitabh Bachchan
Actor and former member of the Lok Sabha

Icons of Diwali #5
Guru Hargobind Ji

The sixth Sikh Guru, Hargobind Ji, is the object of devotion of Sikhs during Bandi Chhor Divas, a festival that occurs at the same time in the lunar calendar as Diwali. Hargobind Ji was a spiritual leader and a warrior who defended Sikhism and justice.*

Bandi Chhor Divas, or "prisoner release day", celebrates the day Hargobind Ji and 52 princes were released from imprisonment at Gwalior Fort, at the demand of Mughal Emperor Jahangir, in 1619. During Diwali, Sikhs often chant "Waheguru, Waheguru" to praise God.

* In Sikhism, Gurus are revered as enlightened teachers but not as divine beings. Sikhs believe in one formless god (Waheguru), beyond human form.

"

Diwali should be celebrated unanimously throughout the world as a gesture of goodwill. It not only belongs to Hinduism but is universal in nature and in its essence too. Diwali ignites the values of self-confidence, love for humanity, peace, prosperity and – above all – eternity, which goes beyond all mortal factors.

"

Julia Roberts*
American actress

* A famous convert to "Hollywood Hinduism" in 2010, along with other notable
  names, including Will Smith, Steve Jobs, Robert Downey Jr. and Madonna.

Britain's first, largest and most authentic Hindu temple, in Neasden, northwest London, is the awe-inspiring BAPS Shri Swaminarayan Mandir, built in 1995. It was famously erected entirely using ancient principles of Hindu architecture and traditional materials, such as Italian marble and Bulgarian limestone*, Indian granite and intricately hand-carved wood. The temple was designed and built by Pramukh Swami, a 92-year-old Indian *sadhu*, or Holy Man. Every year, the temple hosts a large Diwali celebration, with more than 20,000 in attendance.

* 2,828 tonnes of Bulgarian limestone and 2,000 tonnes of Italian marble, to be precise. It was first shipped to India to be carved by a team of 1,526 sculptors!

"

Sometimes I like to knock
on a neighbour's door and go,
'Here's your Christmas card.
I notice you didn't get me one for
Diwali – see you later!'

"

Romesh Ranganathan
British comedian and presenter

CHAPTER
FOUR

Inner Light

From Amavasya to Sivakasi,
rangoli to uphaar, Buddha
to Vishnu, Diwali is a feast of
trivia and traditions, history
and icons.

Let's eradicate the darkness
and dive even deeper into all that's
delicious about Diwali...

"

O Kārtikeya, on the thirteenth day of the dark half of Kārtika, a man should offer a light to Rama outside his house. Thereby untimely death is avoided. 'May the Sun's son, with Death having a noose in his hand and with his wife, be pleased due to this offering of the light.'

"

Śrī Śiva

Chapter 122, "The Celebration of Dīpāvali", *Padma Purana*, 400 BCE

112

D	Divine
I	Illumination
W	Wealth
A	Aspiration
L	Love
I	Inspiration

Most devotees of Diwali these days now advocate a safe and sustainable celebration, with less focus on exploding dangerous firecrackers and buying new stuff and more on spending time with friends and family. Celebrate Diwali safely this year:

1. Use LED Lights

Reduce air pollution and use eco-friendly LEDs for *diyas*.

2. Recycle Decorations

Don't buy new; reuse or recycle decorations, such as *torans* (door hangings) or *akasha* (lanterns), from previous years' materials. A great way to reduce the environmental impact.

3. No Firecrackers

Firecrackers, especially lots all at once, are terrible for the environment as they release harmful pollutants into the air that can cause respiratory problems.

4. All-Natural *Rangoli*

Make your *rangolis* with colour dyes from all-natural sources such as flowers, spices and vegetables.

5. Buy Local

Purchase Diwali gifts, foods, clothes and items from local shops where possible to reduce the impact of freight and shipping.

Mithai

A Diwali festival without sweets – or *mithai* – is not Diwali. *Mithai* are a mix of candy, snack and dessert that include a vast array of ingredients, such as different flours, milks, milk solids, fermented foods, root vegetables, raw and roasted seeds, seasonal fruits, fruit pastes and dry fruits... anything tasty that can be nibbled throughout the day.

The most famous *mithai* for Diwali are ladoo, barfi, gulab jamun, jalebi, rasgulla, kheer, peda and pineapple sheera, to name a few.

"

The light is not in the stars but in the lamp that burns in our hands.

"

Rabindranath Tagore
Bengali polymath

"

In Gujarat, as a child, I would go to my aunt's house in Rajkot for Diwali, where I would make *rangoli*. For me, it is public art – so I'd make extensive, large-scale, realistic-looking drawings of portraits, landscapes and sometimes, imitations of popular imagery on the street. Now, I live in Goa, and Diwali is different here. The highlight is the day before Diwali, when they burn effigies of Narakasura. It's a very Goan thing. Everybody gathers around these structures, and all night they play loud music and dance, finally burning the effigy around five a.m. on Diwali. The whole point is to burn the structure and through that, burn the evil within you.

"

Hanif Kureishi
Indian artist

"

Celebrating the festival of lights teaches us to be grateful and share our blessings.

"

A.P.J. Abdul Kalam
Scientist and former President of India

"

Allow each lamp you light to bring a smile to your face and to enlighten your soul. Allow the earthen lamp's flame to cleanse your heart, mind and soul. May the Diwali lamps brighten your life and the *rangoli* add more colours to it. May the sound of crackers and sweets bring more glee and cheer. The mirth, merriment and joy of this divine festival surround you for the rest of your life.

"

Shree Shambav
Author

"

Happy Diwali to all my Hindu, Sikh and Jain friends, at home and abroad! Well, to be honest, I don't have any Jain friends, but you take my point.

"

Mehdi Hasan
British-American broadcaster and writer

"

May the light of Diwali
bring you peace,
joy and prosperity.

"

Jacqueline Fernandez
Sri Lankan actress

Every Diwali, Indian forces at the famous Attari-Wagah Border crossing between India and Pakistan – located between Amritsar, India, and Lahore, Pakistan – meet their Pakistani counterparts at the Line of Control to offer *mithai* as a gesture of peace between the two warring nations.

During Eid, the gesture is returned by the Pakistani soldiers, who give sweets to the Indian soldiers. Currently, the nations are maintaining a fragile ceasefire.

Raat bhar diye jalaye,
*Diwali ki raat hai.**

"The night of Diwali is here,
with lamps lit throughout
the night."

* A popular poetic phrase about Diwali, often sung or recited.

The Hanuman

Half-monkey, half-human Hanuman is a Hindu god and the most devoted disciple of Prince Rama. A central figure in the *Ramayana*, Hanuman helps Rama rescue his abducted wife Sita from Ravana, the 10-headed demon king, using his special magical powers, such as *kama-rupin* (shapeshifting) and flight.

During Diwali, Hanuman's strength, selflessness, courage and devotion are celebrated, and he has become a symbol of loyalty and righteousness in Hinduism.

"

So Diwali's like a combination of Christmas, New Year's, Fourth of July and *Star Wars*.

"

Todd Dempsey*
"Home for the Diwalidays", *Outsourced*, 2010

* Todd is told by his Hindu colleagues that, "Diwali is all about the triumph of good over evil, and the beginning of the new year, and it marks the end of the harvest, and it commemorates Lord Rama's glorious return after 14 years of exile and his defeat of the demon king Ravana."

Amritsar, the second-largest city in the Indian state of Punjab, is the spiritual heart of Sikhism. It is here that the world-famous Harmandir Sahib, or Golden Temple, is located. The foundation stone of the Golden Temple was laid on Diwali in 1577.

More than 150,000 people visit the temple every single day, but on Bandi Chor Divas and Diwali the number of visitors increases to more than 500,000! During Diwali the entire temple complex is illuminated with hundreds of thousands of lamps, and fireworks light up the night sky.

35 tonnes

The amount of high-quality gold Hindus bought during Diwali 2024.

Silver similarly saw a 30 per cent increase in sales.

Every Diwali, Niagara Falls – one of the world's fastest, most powerful and most iconic waterfalls in the world – celebrates Diwali for the 1.3 million devotees in Canada.

The large waterfall is illuminated in saffron, white and green (India's flag colours) to mark the occasion, and in 2024 they added some bright gold too. Above the waterfalls a large and loud firework display illuminates the sky.

Diwali is a national holiday in 12 countries:

India, Malaysia, Fiji, Guyana, Mauritius, Myanmar, Nepal, Pakistan, Singapore, Sri Lanka, Suriname, and Trinidad and Tobago.

Mysore Palace

Far from an eyesore, Mysore Palace in Karnataka, southwest India, is not just an UNESCO World Heritage Site bu is perhaps the greatest example of illumination writ large on Diwali. The whole palace – 75 acres! – is beautifully lit up with more than 100,000 *diyas* during the festival. It is considered one of the top 10 places to see Diwali in India, alongside Varanasi's Dashashwamedh Ghat and Jaipur's Nahargarh Fort.

₹4.25 trillion*

The value of Diwali to the Indian economy in 2024. (That's approximately $50 billion!)

This is the highest festive spending in India's history, signifying a tenfold growth from 2019.

* Rupees, India's currency

"

Diwali is the darkest night of the year. And our ancestors have taught us to overcome darkness with light.

"

Harihar D. Naik
Indian Poet

In 2024, for the first time ever, Diwali fireworks* in Delhi – India's capital city – were banned from being sold, kept or used. Over the years, air pollution during Diwali has become so bad that it has resulted in an epidemic of health issues for the 17 million residents.

* Delhi, Haryana, Punjab and Tamil Nadu have also imposed bans on firecrackers.

Diwali Purchases

These are the top 13 purchases Diwali devotees make most during the festive season...

25% – cars & electrical goods
13% – food & groceries
12% – clothes
9% – jewellery
8% – electronics & mobile phones
8% – gift items
6% – cosmetics
4% – dry fruit sweets
4% – furnishing and furniture
3% – home decorations
3% – puja samagri
3% – utensils and kitchen appliances
2% – confectionary & bakery

* Data by Tata Fintech, 2024

Puja Samagri

The term used to describe the collection of items used in Hindu worship rituals, or *puja* for Diwali. These items can include flowers (such as *gulal*, *abir* and *rangoli*), incense (such as *attar* and *ashtagandha* powder), sweets (such as dry fruits, *supari*, cloves and cardamom), photo frames of Ganesha and Lakshmi, and coins. These items are left as offerings for Lakshmi to honour her and invite peace and prosperity into the home.

"

Let Diwali be a gentle reminder that merely lighting a candle on the outside isn't enough. We must also nurture the light within ourselves, facing our struggles with courage and kindness. May we kindle our inner flames and shine brightly from within.

"

Monty Panesar
English international cricketer

"

To British Indians, for whom this festival means so much, I want to express my personal admiration and respect for everything you do for our country. Quite simply, Britain would be a lesser country without your contribution. And with the autumnal nights growing ever longer and darker across Britain, this spectacular festival ushers in a new mood and a new spirit of optimism and joy... this really is a festival that can bring all of us together.

"

Boris Johnson
British prime minister, October 2019

History of Hinduism
(Abridged)

Hinduism is believed to be the oldest religion in the world. Unlike many other religions, Hinduism has no single founder; it developed over centuries through various cultural and philosophical traditions.

Its most sacred texts are *The Vedas*, *Upanishads*, *Bhagavad Gita* and *Ramayana*. Hindus believe in the law of karma (cause and effect) and the cycle of birth, death and rebirth (*samsāra*) and recognize millions of gods and goddesses, with Brahma (the creator), Vishnu (the preserver) and Shiva (the destroyer) being the holy trinity.

Vikramaditya

The legendary emperor of ancient India, Vikramaditya, whose reign is thought to have taken place between 380 and 415 CE, was believed to have been coronated on the day of Diwali.

Vikramaditya's long reign – the longest of any Indian emperor – was revered for his expansion of his kingdom, as well as being an ideal leader, with a strong sense of justice, bravery, patronage of scholars and love for the arts. For his entire reign, Diwali was celebrated in his honour.

Uphaar

The one thing that Diwali and Christmas have in common is the gift-buying craze they cause. It is customary to exchange gifts – *uphaar* – on Diwali, and while shopping for them might not have been on the minds of people who celebrated the festival of lights thousands of years ago, it has become a part of the modern Diwali.

Icons of Diwali #6
Lord Mahavira

The supreme preacher of Jainism, Lord Mahavira was born Prince Vardhamana in the Bihar state of India around 599 BCE. For Jainists and disciples of Mahavira's teachings, Diwali marks his nirvana, or spiritual awakening, on 15 October 527 BCE, at the age of 72. His enlightenment, or *Kevalnyan*, transformed Prince Vardhamana into Lord Mahavira – the name is from *maha* (great) and *vira* (hero).

Before he died, Mahavira established a community of 14,000 monks and 36,000 nuns, and a wealth of Jainist teachings, including the five principal tenets of Jainism: no violence, no lying, no stealing, no possessions, and chastity.

"

Diwali is not just a festival but a way of celebrating the true homecoming, welcoming your true self to your mind, body and soul. This Diwali, empower someone to enjoy the festival of lights by making their life bright.

"

Vikram Verma
Indian politician

108

In Hinduism the number 108 is considered sacred due to its associations with the 108 names of deities, 108 sacred texts and the body's 108 energy points.

The number represents a wholeness of existence, cosmic energy and a divine connection.* Meditation and mantras are also recited 108 times. Here are 10 (of the 108) mantras in honour of Goddess Lakshmi:

Om Prakrityai Namah – one who embodies the essence of nature.

Om Vikrityai Namah – one who possesses many diverse attributes.

Om Vidyaayai Namah – the embodiment of wisdom.

Om Sarvabhutahitapradaayai Namah –
one who grants the blessings that benefit
all beings.

Om Shraddhaayai Namah – the
embodiment of devotion.

Om Vibhuutyai Namah – the personification
of opulence.

Om Surabhyai Namah – one with the divine
and celestial entity.

Om Paramaatmikaayai Namah – one who
is present everywhere.

Om Vaache Namah – one who speaks
with a voice as sweet as nectar.

Om Padmaalayaayai Namah – one who
dwells upon the lotus.

* 108 is also the number of the emergency services telephone number in India.

145

World Festivals of Light

18 October – Swanti & Tihar, Newar and Nepali version of Diwali

5 November – Guy Fawkes Night, UK

15 November – Loy Krathong, Thailand

7 December – Day of the Little Candles, Catholic, Colombia

8 December – Fête des lumières, France (Lyon)

13 December – St Lucy's Day, Christian

13 December – Karthika Deepam, Hinduism (Tamil)

14 December (2025) – Hanukkah, Jewish

26 December – Kwanzaa, African-American

2 February – Candlemas, Christian

3 February – Sharjah Light Festival, UAE

12 February – Lantern Parade, Chinese

End of Rainy Season – Tazaungdaing, Buddhist (Myanmar)

30 April – Walpurgis Night, Germany

"

What better place to celebrate the festival of lights than in the crossroads of the world. I'm proud to be with our Hindu brothers and sisters today for the annual Diwali at Times Square celebration, as we push away the darkness and welcome the light all across our city.

"

Eric Adams
New York City Mayor

In 2025, New York's world-famous Times Square will celebrate its 10th Diwali, a festival that showcases the "Colours of India and America", featuring dance performances from different states of India and other ethnic communities like Indo-Caribbean, Africa and Mexico. The *diya* lighting ceremony is synchronized with the countdown on the One Times Square tower, and more than 500,000 people in attendance watch the tourist hotspot light up with Diwali celebrations.

Icons of Diwali #7
Siddhartha Gautama

Born in Lumbini, Nepal, in 563 BCE, Siddhartha Gautama's teachings became the foundation of Buddhism. It also led to his nickname – "Buddha", a word which comes from the Sanskrit root *budh* meaning "to wake up". Gautama's path to enlightenment uncovered the central tenets of Buddhism, known as The Four Noble Truths:

Dukkha: Life is suffering

Samudaya: Suffering is caused by craving

Nirodha: Suffering can end

Magga: There is a path to end suffering

70 per cent of Indians will spend more on clothes, gold, gifts and food this Diwali than they did last Diwali.

CHAPTER
FIVE

Diyas of Our Lives

Diwali is anything but an ordinary celebration – it is unlike any other holy holiday in the world.

Don't believe us?

Turn the page.

The 13th Day

Diwali is celebrated on the 13th day of Diwali's lunar month, Kartika, in October/ November. The 13th is an important day for Hindus, and many cultures around the world. In Hinduism, 13-day rituals known as *Terahvin* and *Pind Sammelan* honour the deceased and mark the end of mourning. Similar mourning rituals can be seen in Buddhism, known as the 13 Days Ceremony.

In Western culture, however, the 13th is considered unlucky, a superstition that may have originated from Norse mythology. The unluckiest may even have *triskaidekaphobia*– a fear of the number 13.

"

Light the lamp of knowledge to dispel ignorance. Light the lamp of compassion to dispel cruelty. Light the lamp of friendliness to dispel animosity. Be light unto yourself and the world.

"

Ravi Shankar
Indian sitarist and composer

"

Within you is the light
of a thousand suns; let
the awakening of this
light guide you to a new
understanding of yourself.

"

Deepak Chopra
Indian-American author, new-age guru and
alternative-medicine advocate.

Anar

A popular type of Diwali firework is the cone-shaped *anar*, also known as a fountain. When lit, it emits a dazzling display of colourful sparks. Unfortunately, the *anar* was found to be responsible for 65 per cent of firework injuries, such as minor burns, during Diwali.

75% potassium nitrate
15% charcoal
10% sulphur

The three ingredients of firecrackers, the popular flash-bangs of light on Diwali night. These ingredients are known by another term: gunpowder.

Before the ban in 2024, more than five million tonnes of firecrackers were burnt during Diwali in Delhi.

City of Lights

The spiritual heart of India and Hinduism, the holy city of Varanasi is one of the world's oldest continuously inhabited cities, dating back more than 3,000 years.

The city is also known as the City of Lights due to it being the first place that the divine light of Lord Shiva pierced through the primordial darkness.

The city is also famed for being located on the sacred Ganges River, which is believed to wash away sins.

"

The light within you is
brighter than the darkness
around you. Let it guide you.

"

Matshona Dhliwayo
Philosopher

On *Dhanteras*, the lighting of the first *diyas* is a family ritual, marking the beginning of Diwali. It is usually done just after sunset in a period known as *Pradosh Kaal*. It is common for the eldest member of the family to lead the ceremony, and some rituals include lighting 13 *diyas* and placing them strategically around the house, such as on windows or rooftops, for protection and to ward off evil spirits.

Diwali Dad Jokes

Don't be a dim bulb this Diwali with your family, make them LOL with these terrible Diwali dad jokes...

What did the light bulb say to the candle on Diwali?
"I'm really delighted to meet you!"

Diwali makes everything light... including my wallet!

Why was the cracker so good
at its job?
It always had a blast.

Why did the *diya* blush?
It saw the firecracker flash.

Why do firecrackers make
good teachers?
They always leave a mark.

There are many types of fireworks popular on Diwali. From *phuljhadi* (sparklers) to wheel-like ground spinners called *chakkars*, rockets to comets and flower pots to "Lakshmi bombs".

Seventy per cent of all Diwali fireworks in India are made in just one location – the southern Indian town of Sivakasi, located in the state of Tamil Nadu. More than 25,000 people work all year round in the town to ensure the nation has enough fireworks for Diwali.

"

With the lighting of the *diyas*, let this be a moment we can look to the future with hope. As a symbol of the triumph of light over darkness, I believe Diwali is a poignant representation of the endeavour for a brighter tomorrow. As your first British Asian Prime Minister, and a devout Hindu, I also hope this can be a celebration of the fantastic ethnic and cultural diversity which makes the UK the place it is today.

"

Rishi Sunak

The speech he made on his first Diwali in office as Great Britain's prime minister, 2022

Diwali & Chill

Diwali is a great opportunity to get together with your loved ones and watch all the latest Bollywood blockbusters.

These movies are set during Diwali, or have pivotal scenes related to the festival, and are a mix of classics and contemporaries...

1. *Mohabbatein* (2000)

2. *Ae Dil Hai Mushkil* (2016)

3. *Kabhi Khushi Kabhie Gham...* (2001)

4. *Vaastav* (1999)

5. *Dilwale Dulhania Le Jayenge* (1995)

6. *Prem Ratan Dhan Payo* (2015)

7. *Om Shanti Om* (2007)

8. *Yeh Jawaani Hai Deewani* (2013)

9. *Kuch Kuch Hota Hai* (1998)

10. *Goliyon Ki Raasleela Ram-Leela* (2013)

Diwali of the Gods

Celebrated in Varanasi, Uttar Pradesh, India, Dev Deepavali – or "Diwali of the Gods" – takes place 15 days after Diwali on the sacred steps of the Ganges River bank. It is a festival that honours Lord Shiva, following his triumph over the demon Tripurasura. Impressed with his victory over darkness, all the Hindu gods descend from Heaven to celebrate – and bathe in the Ganges!

More than a million *diyas* are lit in honour of Lord Shiva and the Ganges and set to float upon the river.

On the day of Diwali 2024, International Space Station (ISS) commander Sunita Williams spoke to President Joe Biden at Washington's White House... while floating 250 miles above the Earth! Her message to her fellow Earthlings was poignant.

"

On this day, I specifically think about my father, who immigrated to the U.S. from India. He kept and shared his cultural roots by teaching us about Diwali and other Indian festivals. Diwali is a time of joy, as goodness in the world prevails. I am so thankful to have grown up in a multicultural household where our parents encouraged us to seek opportunities and reach for the stars.

"

In Hindu mythology, Goddess Lakshmi is often depicted siting on a lotus leaf showing her four hands.

These hands represent the four primary goals of human life:

Dharma — righteousness
Artha — wealth
Kama — desire
Moksha — freedom

Lakshmi is worshipped every day in Hinduism but especially during Diwali, as it is believed that the goddess visits her devotees' houses to shower them with blessings.

Brahmamuhurta

Known as the "Creator's Hour", *Brahmamuhurta* is a 48-minute window of time, just before dawn, when – according to Hindus – the air is fresh and rich in oxygen and filled with serenity, pure vibrations and immense spiritual energy.

It is usually between 3:30 am and 5 am.

During Diwali, *Brahmamuhurta* is the perfect time to meditate, recite mantras and feel the energy of a new light and a new day.

"

Light, my light, the world-filling light, the eye-kissing light, heart-sweetening light! Ah, the light dances, my darling, at the centre of my life; the light strikes, my darling, the chords of my love; the sky opens, the wind runs wild, laughter passes over the earth.

"

Rabindranath Tagore
Bengali polymath

"

At Diwali, my family do just a small *puja*, led by the elders of the family. We dress up, meet friends and have a good time. Diwali is about spending time with family and loved ones, being thankful for the year that has gone by and praying for a better one next year. I think this festival transcends religion; it's the big Indian festival. Of course, things are getting more commercial now. But the essence of Diwali remains.

"

Adil Hussain
Indian actor

" "

Don't fight the darkness – bring the light, and the darkness will disappear.

Maharishi Mahesh Yogi
Creator of Transcendetal Meditation

"

Let's celebrate the festival of lights with a heart full of gratitude and a spirit of togetherness.

"

Nish Kumar
British comedian and television presenter

Light up a loved one's
life this Diwali!

"

Happiness can be found,
even in the darkest of times,
if one only remembers to
turn on the light.

"

J.K. Rowling
British author

60 per cent

The percentage increase the search term "Diwali celebration" has grown year-on-year in the U.S., suggesting that Diwali, and Diwali parties, are on their way to becoming one of America's mainstream and commercial cultural events, such as Halloween and Thanksgiving.

4.4 million

The number of people with Indian origins who reside in America, many of whom celebrate Diwali!

Playlist:
Classic Songs About Light

Shine a light on your music this Diwali
with a little illumination...

1. "The Inner Light" – The Beatles

2. "Light My Fire" – The Doors

3. "Shine a Light" – The Rolling Stones

4. "Love Is Eternal Sacred Light" – Paul Simon

5. "Blinded by the Lights" – The Weeknd

6. "Beginning to See the Light" – The Velvet
Underground

7. "Guiding Light" – Mumford & Sons

8. "Let There Be Light" – Hillsong Worship

9. "Heading for the Light" – Traveling Wilburys

10. "There Is a Light That Never Goes Out" –
The Smiths

178

50,000 tonnes (100 million pounds)

The amount of fireworks exploded annually in India during Diwali celebrations – before the start of firework bans in 2024.

India has given more light to the world than just Diwali. Its many languages have famously contributed to the English language with a feast of fantastic words we still use every day.

Here are our favourite:

Bāṅdhnū – Bandana
Vilāyatī/Bilātī – Blighty
Baṅglā – Bungalow

Kashmir – Cashmere
Caṭnī – Chutney
Khāṭ – Cot
Ḍiṅgī – Dinghy
Jagannāth – Juggernaut
Jaṅgala – Jungle
Paṇḍit – Pundit
Paijāmā – Pyjamas
Śāṭī – Sari
Chāmpo – Shampoo
Shāl – Shawl

Shakti and Bhakti

Hinduism encourages a combination of its two most important values – *shakti* and *bhakti*. *Shakti* means "strength" or "power', while *bhakti* is "devotion" or "worship".

A good Hindu is strong and powerful but should only use their power in devotion to the gods and to help other people, rather than solely for themselves.

"

Choose light always, whatever the future may bring. Whatever the future may bring, it is our light and our fierce commitment to one another that will see us through to a better day. That is the message of Diwali.

"

Vivek Murthy
Physician and former United States Surgeon General

Deepapratipadutsava

One of the earliest written references to Diwali as a festival was recorded in the Sanskrit play by the name of *Nagananda*, written during the reign of Emperor Harsha in the seventh century. It was around this time that the shortened word "Diwali" became a household name.

Deepa = light
Pratipada = first day
Utsava = festival

Tilak

On the fifth and final day of festivities, Bhai Dooj, sisters initiate a *tilak* ceremony whereby a red dot – made from a paste of ash, sandalwood, turmeric, clay or vermillion – is placed on a brother's forehead.

The *tilak* ("mark") symbolizes a renewed sense of spiritual awareness for the new year.

The Noble Eightfold Path

Also known as the Middle Way, the Noble Eightfold Path is a set of eight interconnected principles that guide Buddhists toward a state of wisdom and ethical enlightenment.

Do you walk the Path?

1. Right action – behaving in a skilful way and not harming others

2. Right speech – speaking truthfully

3. Right livelihood – earning a living in a way that doesn't cause harm to others

4. Right mindfulness – being aware of yourself and the emotions of others

5. Right effort – putting effort into meditation and positive emotions

6. Right concentration – developing focus so that you are able to meditate

7. Right view/understanding – remembering that actions have consequences

8. Right intention – being clear about following the Buddhist path

Govatsa Dwadashi

To mark the beginning of Diwali in some parts of northern India, Hindus honour cows in a ritual called Govatsa Dwadashi. Cows are the most sacred animal in Hinduism.

In bathing ceremonies, cows and calves are washed and then draped in clothes and flower garlands, and turmeric powder is applied on their foreheads. In some villages, Hindus sculpt cows and calves symbolically out of mud.

"

Doubt everything.
Find your own light.

"

Siddhartha Gautama
The Buddha

"

O Lakshmi, whose heart is full of mercy,
who is worshipped throughout the three
worlds and who is the giver of all fortune
and the mother of Creation. You are the
wonderful energy of Lord Vishnu, who
is maintaining the three worlds. You are
the Supreme Goddess. You are eternal and
deliverer of all fallen souls. All glories unto
You. O Devi, for the welfare and protection
of the three worlds. All glories unto You,
whose glories are unlimited. Kindly be
merciful upon me.

"

Vyasa
The Bhagavad Gita, Chapter 12, 400 BCE

Diwali is about *goals*,
not gold.

The word "Lakshmi", the name given to the goddess of wealth and fortune, is derived from the Sanskrit word *laksya*, meaning "aim" or "goal".

शुभ दीपावली
Shubh Diwali!